The Complete Slow Cooker Cookbook for Family and Friends

Quick and Delicious Recipes for Every Day incl. Side Dishes, Desserts and More

Matthew A. Hammond

Table of Contents

Introduction

What is a Slow Cooker?

Slow cookers, also known as crock pots, are countertop electronic appliances that cook food with gentle heat over longer hours than other cooking methods. Slow cookers are commonly used for stews, soups, and pot roasts, but they can do far more than that. Pasta dishes, appetisers, vegetarian specialties, and even scrumptious desserts can be made with the humble slow cooker – and results can be spectacular.

Why a Slow Cooker?

For delicious, nutritious, and convenient meals that require minimal preparation time, a slow cooker can be an incredible investment. Unlike with baking or frying, slow cooking allows the chef to leave heating food unattended for hours and return later to a fully cooked meal.

Slow cookers were invented in the 1940s and grew in popularity when more women started leaving the home to work. A slow cooker enabled them to both work outside of home and make dinner for the entire family. Ingredients would simply be added to the slow cooker in the morning and dinner would be fully ready by the time they returned home.

Aside from ease and convenience, benefits of slow cooking include:

• Higher energy efficiency.

A slow cooker uses significantly less electricity than a conventional electric oven, making it an excellent option for those looking to lower their electricity bills. In fact, its energy usage is only slightly more than a typical lightbulb. Slow cooker-owners can rest assured that a meal slow-cooked for eight hours or more is not much different from leaving a light on for that same amount of time.

• Better results with cheaper cuts of meat.

When fried or roasted, a cheaper cut of meat can turn out significantly less flavourful or tender than a cut that's more expensive. A slow cooker, on the other hand, can make even a cheap cut of meat taste and feel remarkable. Meat is more likely to dry out when it's cooked quickly, which is why a slow cooker is perfect for ensuring juicy, tender meat. Slow cooker chefs can freely embrace cheaper cuts like pork shoulder, lamb shank, or beef chuck without sacrificing taste or quality.

• Greater preservation of nutrients.

When vegetables and other healthy foods are boiled, baked, or fried, plenty of nutrients are destroyed in the cooking process. Cauliflower, for example, is said to lose over half of its antioxidants when boiled. Slow cooking, on the other hand, preserves most nutrients due to the lower heat used and the machine's tight lid. Since everything is kept within the same tightly covered pot, any nutrients lost are also easily recaptured in the sauce or juices at the bottom of the machine.

• Won't increase the temperature in your kitchen.

Unlike roasting or baking, slow cooking won't heat up your kitchen even if it's on for several hours. This means that even on a hot summer's day, there's nothing holding you back from making a delicious meal in your slow cooker.

• It's a portable machine.

There's no need to go through the trouble of transferring your slow-cooked meal into a casserole dish – even if you're going to a pot-luck. Simply remove the inner pot and cover with the lid, and voila. Many even choose to bring the entire machine, which is easy to plug in at your next location. This ensures that the meal you've brought is nice and hot, no matter the travel time.

Choosing the Right Slow Cooker

There are many factors to consider when choosing the right slow cooker for you and your family. With a wide selection of machines available to you, consider the following before making your final choice.

How many people you're serving

Each time you use your cooker, you'll need to fill up the machine most of the way, so it's important to find a size that works for you and your family. Purchasing a larger machine when you serve only two people most nights will leave you with far more food than you need!

If you're only cooking for yourself or one other person, the ideal slow cooker for you will be between 1.5 to 3 litres. If you're serving a small family of three or four people, choose a machine between 3 and 5 litres. If you're cooking for a large family or would like to have leftovers, the right slow cooker for you will be over 5 litres, with about 6 litres serving six to eight people.

In all cases, when looking for a slow cooker, make sure to find out what the machine's *usable* volume is, as this can sometimes be far less than what the box states.

What type of food you'll be cooking

Slow cookers either come in an oval or round shape, and this difference is not purely aesthetic. Oval slow cookers are a much better choice for bulky foods, which can be difficult to remove from a round cooker. If you're planning on cooking a whole chicken or pork chops, consider an oval slow cooker. Otherwise, consider a round slow cooker, which uses slightly less electricity and has a cheaper price point.

What settings would most help you

Needless to say, the more settings a machine has, the more expensive it will be. However, you may find them worth the extra cost. Some extra features may include a 'keep warm' setting, a timer, or an 'auto cook' function which begins with a high temperature and automatically switches to a low temperature part way through cooking.

Understanding Your Machine

Temperature Settings: An Easy Guide

Low Heat

If you're cooking with a cheaper cut of meat, low heat will achieve perfection in texture and enhance delicious flavours. While this can take as long as 8-10 hours, the result will be more tender and juicier than what you'll achieve in most ovens. Low heat is suitable for most dishes and its use generally depends on how much time is available for cooking.

Medium Heat

Not all slow cookers offer a medium heat option, but it's a safe choice for most cuts of meat. While you won't end up with as tender a result as something cooked on low, you'll still get some of the benefits and in less time. Medium heat is a good choice for a balance of flavour and time efficiency. It's worth noting, however, that medium heat can vary with each machine.

High Heat

Set your machine at high heat if you're cooking poultry such as chicken. This ensures that the meat cooks quickly and evenly. Furthermore, high heat is ideal for dishes with a lot of vegetables as they need more moisture to break down. This is especially true for hard vegetables like carrots, though extra time or added liquid can also solve these issues on lower heat.

How to Get the Best Results with a Slow Cooker

Read the manual

With so many brands of slow cookers, each one varies considerably and may have slightly different features. For this reason, it's important that you get to know your machine by reading the manual. This will ensure you get the best results with every meal you cook. Cooking time will vary depending on your exact model.

Keep the lid on while it's cooking

It's tempting to pull the lid off the slow cooker so you can get a whiff of your delicious meal, but try not to do this unless the recipe specifically asks you to do so. Removing the lid will let cool air into the machine and this can slow down the cooking process.

Put the right amount of food into the slow cooker

It's important to not under-fill or overfill your slow cooker so that your meal can cook properly. The exact amount of food or liquid to place inside will depend on your slow cooker, but it should be no more than three-quarters of the way full. Make sure to adjust the serving size of every recipe if it does not suit the size of your machine.

Preheat your machine before cooking

When it comes to slow cooking, one of the most overlooked steps is preheating. Don't turn the cooker on only after you've placed the ingredients inside; always do it at least 10 minutes before. The amount of cook time lost may seem negligible to you, but it may have an effect on your meal. As with all other cooking methods, an extra 10-15 minutes can make a lot of difference to texture and flavour.

Don't forget your food!

One of the many benefits of a slow cooker is being able to forget it for a few hours. However, it's important to not forget it altogether. Leaving slow-cooked food longer than the recipe asks can still leave you with a burnt or, at the very least, dry meal. To prevent this, set a timer and make sure to check on your meal when it needs your attention.

How to Make Delicious Meals

Slow Cooker Tips for Perfect Food Preparation

Trim the fat from all fatty cuts of meat

When meat is fried, any fat on the meat is easily drained from the pan after cooking. Meat in the slow cooker, however, is a different story. Leaving meat untrimmed can result in fat rising to the top or an unsightly pool of grease at the bottom. Trim your meat and the results will not only be tastier and nicer to look at, but also much more healthy.

Only slow cook skinless chicken

Whatever the cut of chicken, make sure it's skinless before you leave it to cook in your slow cooker. Frying or baking skin-on chicken may result in a lovely, crispy skin but slow cooking exposes chicken to wet heat for many hours, resulting in a rubbery texture that is much less appetising.

Use the excess liquid

If you do end up with excess liquid at the bottom of your slow cooker, don't get rid of it. Simply gather the liquid and combine with flour or cornstarch, then season well with salt and pepper. This is an easy way to make a delicious gravy to pair perfectly with your meal. If the liquid is unusable, leave the machine uncovered on high heat for several minutes to let the excess moisture evaporate.

Always rinse the starch from rice

People tend to skip the rinse stage when it comes to making rice, but rinsing leads to far better results when you're cooking rice in a slow cooker. If fluffy rice sounds more appealing to you than a sticky clump, then always make sure to rinse the excess starch from your rice grains. It only takes a few minutes and can make a world of difference to your meal.

Put pasta in the cooker near the end

You'll notice that every pasta recipe in this book asks you to make the pasta separately on the stovetop or to add it 20-30 minutes before cooking time is complete. There's a good reason for this! Pasta that's been sitting in hot moisture for too long runs the risk of being overcooked. To prevent pasta turning out soggy or mushy, ensure it's not exposed to heat and water for too long.

Recipes

Appetisers & Soup

SPINACH & ARTICHOKE DIP

MAKES 12 SERVINGS
SETTING: LOW | PREP TIME: 10 MINUTES | COOK TIME: 2.5 HOURS

PER SERVING
CARBS: 8.8G | PROTEIN: 10.4G | FIBRE: 3.2G | FAT: 20.6G
KCAL: 252

INGREDIENTS

- 500g artichoke hearts (1 can)
- 400g spinach
- 400g cream cheese
- 300ml plain Greek yoghurt or sour cream
- 100g shredded mozzarella or cheddar cheese
- 100g grated parmesan cheese
- 2 garlic cloves
- 1 red onion

INSTRUCTIONS

1. Dice the red onion and mince the garlic. Chop the artichoke into quarters if they are not quartered already.
2. Add all of the ingredients including the chopped vegetables to the slow cooker. Season well with salt and black pepper. Stir to combine.
3. Cover and cook on low for 2 hours.
4. Stir to mix around the cream cheese.
5. Cook for an additional 30 minutes.
6. Serve with French bread or crackers.

CHICKEN MOZZARELLA MEATBALLS

MAKES 8 SERVINGS
SETTING: HIGH | PREP TIME: 15 MINUTES | COOK TIME: 3 HOURS

PER SERVING
CARBS: 11.5G | PROTEIN: 32G | FIBRE: 1.9G | FAT: 16.4G
KCAL: 326

INGREDIENTS

- 800g chopped tomatoes (2 cans)
- 450g ground chicken
- 350g mozzarella balls (drained)
- 60ml red wine
- 60g grated parmesan cheese
- 60g breadcrumbs
- 3 garlic cloves
- 1 large egg
- 1 medium onion
- ½ tsp basil
- ½ tsp oregano

INSTRUCTIONS

1. Dice the onion and garlic.
2. Add the red wine, diced garlic, onion, and chopped tomatoes to the slow cooker. Season with salt, pepper, and basil.
3. In a large mixing bowl, combine the ground chicken, grated parmesan, egg, and breadcrumbs. Season with salt, pepper, and oregano.
4. Once combined, flatten about 1 tablespoon of the chicken mixture onto a chopping board or other clean surface. Add a mozzarella ball to the center of the flattened meat. Carefully pull the meat up and wrap around the cheese. Roll into a ball.
5. Repeat with the remaining chicken and mozzarella.
6. Place the rolled meatballs into the slow cooker. Cover and cook on high for 3 hours.
7. Serve with any extra parmesan or basil.

CHORIZO Y QUESO FUNDIDO

MAKES 12 SERVINGS
SETTING: HIGH | PREP TIME: 10 MINUTES | COOK TIME: 2 HOURS

PER SERVING
CARBS: 4.5G | PROTEIN: 20.9G | FIBRE: 0.9G | FAT: 29.9G
KCAL: 371

INGREDIENTS

- 500g chorizo
- 500g gouda or mild cheddar cheese
- 300g diced tomatoes (¾ can)
- 2 jalapeno peppers
- 2 onions
- ½ lime
- 2 tsps coriander

INSTRUCTIONS

1. Dice the chorizo, onions and jalapeno peppers. Grate the cheese.
2. In a skillet over medium heat, cook the diced chorizo until it's browned and slightly crispy.
3. Drain the diced tomatoes of water then add to a bowl. Combine with the diced jalapeno, onions, and coriander. Squeeze in the juice of half a lime then mix together. This is your salsa mixture.
4. Add the diced chorizo, salsa mixture, and all the shredded cheese to the slow cooker. Season with salt and pepper, then stir.
5. Cover and cook on high for 2 hours.
6. Serve with tortilla chips or toasted bread.

BROCCOLI & CHEESE SOUP

MAKES 6 SERVINGS
SETTING: HIGH | PREP TIME: 10 MINUTES | COOK TIME: 4 HOURS

PER SERVING
CARBS: 17.6G | PROTEIN: 21.8G | FIBRE: 3.1G | FAT: 36.2G
KCAL: 477

INGREDIENTS

- 900ml vegetable broth
- 250ml double cream
- 350g grated cheddar cheese
- 50g all-purpose flour
- 2 medium heads broccoli
- 2 carrots
- 1 yellow onion

INSTRUCTIONS

1. Dice the onion and chop the broccoli into bite-sized florets. With a boxed grater, shred the carrots. Add all chopped vegetables to the slow cooker.
2. In a bowl, whisk the vegetable broth and the flour until combined. Pour into the slow cooker.
3. Season with salt and pepper, then cover with the lid and cook on high for 3-4 hours.
4. Shortly before cooking time is up, remove the lid from the slow cooker. Add the double cream and grated cheese. Stir to combine.
5. Cook for an additional 15 minutes.
6. Serve alone or with bread for dipping.

CHICKEN POT PIE SOUP

MAKES 6 SERVINGS
SETTING: HIGH | PREP TIME: 10 MINUTES | COOK TIME: 5 HOURS

PER SERVING
CARBS: 52.7G | PROTEIN: 45G | FIBRE: 6.9G | FAT: 21.4G
KCAL: 583

INGREDIENTS

- 1.2kg chicken broth
- 700g boneless chicken breasts
- 250g baking potatoes
- 100g corn
- 100g peas
- 60g all-purpose flour
- 60g butter
- 2 large potatoes
- 2 medium carrots
- 1 yellow onion
- 3 tbsps heavy cream
- 1 tbsp garlic powder
- 1 tsp oregano

INSTRUCTIONS

1. Cube the potatoes into small pieces. Dice the carrots and onion. Add the chopped vegetables into the slow cooker with the corn and peas.
2. Slice the chicken breasts into bite-sized pieces. Add to the slow cooker.
3. Pour in the chicken broth. Season with salt, pepper, garlic powder, and oregano.
4. Cover and cook on high for 3-4 hours.
5. About 2 hours into cooking time, heat the butter in a saucepan over medium heat.
6. Once melted, add flour and stir constantly to create a smooth paste.
7. Add the flour and butter paste to the slow cooker. Stir to combine until it dissolves into the broth.
8. Cook for 1 more hour.
9. Once cooking is finished, add the heavy cream to the soup.
10. Mix together and serve.

MINESTRONE

MAKES 6 SERVINGS
SETTING: LOW, HIGH | PREP TIME: 5 MINUTES | COOK TIME: 8 HOURS 20 MINUTES

PER SERVING
CARBS: 112G | PROTEIN: 42.3G | FIBRE: 31.1G | FAT: 4.7G
KCAL: 643

INGREDIENTS

- 900ml vegetable broth
- 400g chopped tomatoes (1 can)
- 400g red kidney beans (1 can)
- 400g cannellini beans (1 can)
- 150g green beans
- 150g ditalini pasta or macaroni
- 60g spinach
- 50g grated parmesan cheese
- 2 tbsps tomato paste
- 4 garlic cloves
- 2 medium carrots
- 2 stalks celery
- 1 courgette
- 1 white onion
- 1 bay leaf
- 1 tsp oregano

INSTRUCTIONS

1. Dice the garlic and onion. Slice the green beans and celery stalks. Quarter-slice the courgette and carrots. Add all the chopped vegetables to the slow cooker.

2. Add the remaining ingredients into the slow cooker except for the kidney beans, cannellini beans, spinach, and pasta. Season well with salt and pepper.

3. Cover and cook on low for 7-8 hours.

4. Drain the cans of kidney beans and cannellini beans. Pour contents into the slow cooker followed by the pasta and spinach.

5. Cover and cook on high for 20 minutes or until pasta is cooked.

6. Serve with any remaining parmesan cheese.

Red-Meat Main Courses

CLASSIC BREAKFAST CASSEROLE

MAKES 8 SERVINGS
SETTING: LOW | PREP TIME: 10 MINUTES | COOK TIME: 7 HOURS

PER SERVING
CARBS: 36.3G | PROTEIN: 31.1G | FIBRE: 3.2G | FAT: 45.4G
KCAL: 678

INGREDIENTS

- 750g hash browns
- 350g shredded cheddar cheese
- 220ml milk
- 16 slices bacon
- 12 eggs
- 1 spring onion
- ½ yellow onion
- ½ tsp garlic powder
- ¼ tsp mustard

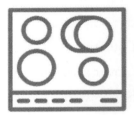

INSTRUCTIONS

1. In a skillet, arrange the bacon in a single layer and cook over medium-high heat.
2. While the bacon cools, dice the yellow onion and finely slice the spring onion.
3. Chop the bacon into bite-sized pieces.
4. Layer half of the hash browns onto the bottom of a greased slow cooker followed by half of the diced yellow onions. Create another layer with half of the shredded cheese and half of the cooked bacon bits. Repeat once more.
5. In a bowl, whisk the eggs with milk, garlic powder, mustard, salt, and pepper.
6. Pour the egg mixture into the slow cooker as the final layer.
7. Cover and cook on low for 7 hours.
8. Serve with a topping of sliced spring onions.

PORK RAGU PASTA

MAKES 6 SERVINGS
SETTING: HIGH | PREP TIME: 20 MINUTES | COOK TIME: 5 HOURS

PER SERVING
CARBS: 13.5G | PROTEIN: 48.9G | FIBRE: 3.2G | FAT: 10.5G
KCAL: 359

INGREDIENTS

- 1kg boneless pork shoulder
- 800g chopped tomatoes (2 cans)
- 600g pappardelle or fettuccine pasta
- 150ml chicken broth
- 100ml red wine
- 50g grated parmesan cheese
- 5 garlic cloves
- 3 medium carrots
- 1 onion
- 1 bay leaf
- 2 tbsps tomato paste
- 1 tbsp olive oil
- 1 tsp sugar
- 1 tsp thyme
- 1 tsp oregano

INSTRUCTIONS

1. Mince the garlic. Finely dice the carrots and onion. Slice the pork shoulder into big chunks.
2. Heat a large pan with olive oil over medium-high heat. Add the chopped pork to the pan. Season well with salt and pepper. Cook until the meat is lightly browned, about 2-3 minutes on each side.
3. Add the chopped onions to the pan. Cook for 3-4 minutes until softened and translucent.
4. Add the garlic and chopped onions. Stir and cook for another 1-2 minutes until the garlic is fragrant.
5. Pour the wine into the pan and allow to boil for 5 minutes.
6. Stir in the chopped tomatoes, tomato paste, chicken broth, sugar, thyme, and oregano. Season again with salt and pepper. Stir well and bring to a simmer.
7. Transfer everything to the slow cooker. Add the bay leaf.
8. Cover and cook on high for 4 to 5 hours.
9. Shortly before the ragu is cooked, boil a pot of water and cook the pasta according to the package instructions.
10. Remove the bay leaf from the slow cooker. Shred the cooked pork with two forks.
11. Top the pasta with the pork ragu sauce.
12. Serve with grated parmesan cheese.

BEEF STEW

MAKES 6 SERVINGS
SETTING: LOW, HIGH | PREP TIME: 20 MINUTES |
COOK TIME: 7 HOURS 15 MINUTES

PER SERVING
CARBS: 27.9G | PROTEIN: 65.8G | FIBRE: 4.7G | FAT: 15.9G
KCAL: 555

INGREDIENTS

- 1.2kg beef chuck
- 450g potatoes
- 400ml beef broth
- 200ml red wine
- 100g peas
- 30g all-purpose flour
- 5 garlic cloves
- 5 medium carrots
- 1 onion
- 1 bay leaf
- 2 tbsps tomato paste
- 1 tbsp olive oil
- 2 tsps Italian seasoning
- 1 tsp balsamic vinegar

INSTRUCTIONS

1. Dice the onion and garlic. Quarter-slice the carrots and chop the potatoes into bite-sized chunks. Chop the beef chuck into pieces about 2-3cm in width and length.

2. Heat a pan with olive oil over medium-high heat. Add the chopped beef chuck to the pan. Season with salt and pepper. Cook for 4-5 minutes or until the beef is nicely browned.

3. Transfer the cooked beef to a greased slow cooker. Add the broth, red wine, tomato paste, vinegar, potatoes, carrots, bay leaf, garlic, and onion. Season with salt, pepper, and Italian seasoning.

4. Cover with the lid and cook on low for 7 hours.

5. With a heat-safe glass or cup, remove about 100ml of broth from the slow cooker. Having the exact amount isn't necessary, it just needs to be roughly half of a drinking glass.

6. Whisk flour into the water until smooth. Pour back into the slow cooker and stir gently. Add the peas.

7. Do not put the lid back on the slow cooker. Cook on high for 15 minutes or until the broth looks thicker.

8. Serve alone or with toasted bread.

HONEY-GARLIC PORK ROAST

MAKES 8 SERVINGS
SETTING: LOW | PREP TIME: 10 MINUTES | COOK TIME: 10 HOURS 20 MINUTES

PER SERVING
CARBS: 25.6G | PROTEIN: 66.6G | FIBRE: 1.2G | FAT: 20.9G
KCAL: 564

INGREDIENTS

- 2kg boneless pork shoulder*
- 200ml chicken broth
- 200g honey
- 100g butter
- 50ml apple cider vinegar
- 3 carrots
- 3 stalks celery
- 2 garlic cloves
- 2 tsps cornstarch
- 1 onion
- 1 tbsp olive oil
- 1 tbsp sage
- 1 tsp thyme
- 1 bay leaf

* Can be substituted with pork loin, but in this case, halve cooking time to 5 hours.

INSTRUCTIONS

1. Chop the onion into eighths, mince the garlic, and quarter-slice the carrots. Cut the celery into pieces of about 4cm in length.

2. In a small bowl, combine about a teaspoon of the olive oil with sage, thyme, salt, and pepper. Rub all over the pork.

3. Heat the rest of the olive oil in a large skillet over medium-high heat. Add the pork and sear until the meat is well browned, about 3 minutes on each side. Once finished, transfer the pork to the slow cooker.

4. Add butter and garlic to the empty skillet. Cook until fragrant and golden then add the honey and vinegar. Season with salt and pepper. Stir and allow to simmer for about 30-45 seconds.

5. Add the onions, carrots, celery, and bay leaf to the slow cooker.

6. Pour the honey-garlic sauce over the pork and vegetables.

7. Cover and cook on low for 10 hours.

8. Remove the cooked pork and allow to rest for 10-15 minutes wrapped in foil.

9. In the meantime, pour the juices in the slow cooker into a pot and bring to a boil. Make sure to remove the bay leaf.

10. Dissolve the cornstarch into two tablespoons of cold water.

11. Reduce heat and bring the juices to a simmer. Add the cornstarch and water mixture. Whisk to combine then leave to simmer for about 4-5 minutes until thickened. Season with salt.

12. Slice the pork shoulder into pieces of about 1.5cm in width.

13. Serve the pork roast and vegetables with sauce on top or on the side.

BEEF STROGANOFF

MAKES 8 SERVINGS
SETTING: LOW | PREP TIME: 10 MINUTES | COOK TIME: 5 HOURS

PER SERVING
CARBS: 49G | PROTEIN: 46.3G | FIBRE: 2.7G | FAT: 26.4G
KCAL: 639

INGREDIENTS

- 900g beef silverside
- 450g flat egg noodles
- 240g sour cream
- 200ml beef broth
- 200ml white wine
- 200g mushrooms
- 150g cream cheese (softened)
- 40g all-purpose flour
- 1 onion
- 1 tbsp Worcestershire sauce

INSTRUCTIONS

1. Prepare by dicing the onion and slicing the mushrooms. Chop the beef into cubes of about 3cm.

2. In the greased slow cooker, add the cubed beef, Worcestershire sauce, white wine, sliced mushrooms, and onions. Add most of the beef broth, but reserve roughly 50ml. Season with salt and lots of black pepper. Stir to fully combine.

3. Cover and cook on low for 5 hours.

4. About 30 minutes before cook time is complete, whisk together the flour, cream cheese, sour cream, and the remaining beef broth. Gently stir into the slow cooker.

5. Do not cover with the lid. Cook for 30 minutes on high.

6. Prepare the egg noodles according to the package instructions.

7. Serve the creamy beef sauce over egg noodles and enjoy.

LAMB SHAWARMA

MAKES 8 SERVINGS
SETTING: HIGH | PREP TIME: 20 MINUTES | COOK TIME: 5 HOURS

PER SERVING
CARBS: 35.6G | PROTEIN: 65.2G | FIBRE: 3.2G | FAT: 22.9G
KCAL: 623

INGREDIENTS

For the wrap:

- 2kg lamb shoulder
- 8-10 large wraps or flatbread pieces
- 300ml beef or lamb broth
- 100ml water
- 250g shredded lettuce
- 3 garlic cloves
- 2 Roma tomatoes
- 1 small cucumber
- 3 tbsps olive oil
- 2 tbsps lemon juice
- 1 tbsp cumin
- 1 tbsp coriander
- 1 tsp paprika

For the sauce:

- 300ml plain Greek yoghurt
- 2 garlic cloves
- 1 tbsp chopped mint
- 1 tbsp dill
- 2 tsps lemon juice

INSTRUCTIONS

1. Mince 3 garlic cloves.

2. In a bowl, combine the minced garlic, olive oil, lemon juice, cumin, coriander, and paprika. Mix until it forms a paste then lather all over the lamb shoulder.

3. Add the broth and water to the slow cooker. Carefully insert the lamb shoulder. Season with salt and pepper.

4. Cover and cook on high for 5 hours.

5. Meanwhile, mince the last 2 garlic cloves. Chop the tomatoes and cucumber into small quarter-slices.

6. In a small bowl mix together the yoghurt, minced garlic, chopped mint, dill, lemon juice, salt and pepper. Cool in the fridge until the lamb is cooked.

7. Slice or shred the cooked lamb and feel free to mix with any of the leftover juices in the slow cooker.

8. Arrange the shawarma by filling each wrap with lamb, minted yoghurt, shredded lettuce, chopped tomatoes, and cucumber.

9. Roll into neat wraps and serve.

SPAGHETTI BOLOGNESE

MAKES 6 SERVINGS
SETTING: LOW | PREP TIME: 40 MINUTES | COOK TIME: 6 HOURS

PER SERVING
CARBS: 74G | PROTEIN: 32.3G | FIBRE: 5.6G | FAT: 21.4G
KCAL: 645

INGREDIENTS

- 750g ground beef
- 800g chopped tomatoes (2 cans)
- 500g spaghetti pasta
- 200ml milk
- 200ml red wine*
- 150g grated parmesan cheese
- 1 yellow onion

- 1 medium carrot
- 3 garlic cloves
- 2 tbsps tomato paste
- 2 tbsps olive oil
- ½ tsp thyme
- ½ tsp oregano
- 1 bay leaf

* Can be substituted with beef broth.

INSTRUCTIONS

1. Mince the garlic. Dice the onion and carrot.

2. Heat olive oil in a large skillet over medium-high heat. Cook the carrots and onions until softened, about 3-4 minutes. Season with salt. Add the onions and cook for 1 more minute until fragrant.

3. Transfer the contents of the skillet to the slow cooker, but feel free to keep some of the onions if you would like them to caramelise more.

4. Add another tablespoon of oil to the skillet. Increase to high heat.

5. Add the ground beef to the pan with thyme, oregano, salt, and pepper. Cook until browned, then add the tomato paste and chopped tomatoes.

6. Use your spatula to break up the ground beef so it doesn't cook in clumps. Allow to simmer for about 10 minutes so some of the moisture can be cooked off.

7. Reduce to medium heat. Pour in the milk and simmer for 5 minutes. Add the red wine, stir together, and leave to simmer for 10 minutes. Transfer to the slow cooker once finished.

8. Add the bay leaf to the slow cooker and mix.

9. Cover and cook on low for 5-6 hours.

10. About 20-30 minutes before cooking time is up, begin making the spaghetti. Bring a large pot of salted water to boil and cook the pasta for 2 minutes less than what the package instructions say.

11. Mix pasta into the slow cooker.

12. If, at this point, the sauce looks too soupy, leave it to cook with the lid off so the excess moisture can evaporate.

13. Serve with grated parmesan cheese.

BEEF LASAGNA

MAKES 6 SERVINGS
SETTING: HIGH | PREP TIME: 10 MINUTES | COOK TIME: 4 HOURS

PER SERVING
CARBS: 51.8G | PROTEIN: 45.5G | FIBRE: 1.8G | FAT: 17.6G
KCAL: 560

INGREDIENTS

- 580g Sainsbury's Tomato & Herb Pasta Sauce (2 jars)
- 500g ricotta cheese
- 450g ground beef
- 200g shredded mozzarella cheese
- 50g grated parmesan cheese
- 16 no-boil lasagna sheets (uncooked)
- 1 onion
- 1 tbsp basil
- 1 tsp Italian seasoning
- 1 tsp garlic powder

INSTRUCTIONS

1. Finely dice the onion.

2. In a pan over medium heat, cook the ground beef and chopped onion until the meat is nicely browned, about 3-4 minutes. Drain excess liquid from the pan.

3. Season with salt, pepper, Italian seasoning, and garlic powder. Stir to combine with the meat and onions, then take the pan off the heat.

4. Cover the bottom of the slow cooker with one-quarter of the pasta sauce and top with four lasagna noodles.

5. Spread one-third of the ricotta cheese evenly onto the lasagna sheet in the slow cooker. Top with one-third of the shredded mozzarella and a sprinkle of parmesan.

6. Add a layer of one-third of the ground beef on top of the cheese.

7. Repeat steps 4 to 6 twice more, beginning with a layer of pasta sauce and ending with a layer of ground beef.

8. For the final layers, add the last of the lasagna sheets followed by the last quarter of the pasta sauce and the rest of the mozzarella.

9. Cover and cook on high for 4 hours.

10. Top with parmesan and basil, and serve.

LAMB ROGAN JOSH

MAKES 6 SERVINGS
SETTING: LOW | PREP TIME: 40 MINUTES | COOK TIME: 6 HOURS

PER SERVING
CARBS: 10.5G | PROTEIN: 25.7G | FIBRE: 2G | FAT: 28G
KCAL: 397

INGREDIENTS

- 700g lamb neck
- 400g chopped tomatoes (1 can)
- 250g plain yoghurt
- 4 garlic cloves
- 1 onion
- 1 lamb stock cube
- 1 bay leaf
- 3 tbsps tomato paste

- 3 tbsps olive oil
- 1 tbsp coriander
- 1 ½ tsps garam masala*
- 1 tsp cumin
- 1 tsp paprika
- 1 tsp chilli powder
- 1 tsp ground ginger

* Can be substituted with curry powder.

INSTRUCTIONS

1. Mince the garlic and finely dice the onion.
2. In a bowl, combine the tomato paste, minced garlic, cumin, garam masala, paprika, ground ginger, chilli powder, lamb stock cube, and one tablespoon of olive oil. Season with salt and pepper. Stir to form a paste.
3. Slice the lamb into pieces of about 4cm.
4. Coat the lamb chunks in the spice paste. Leave to marinate for 30 minutes to 2 hours, the longer the better.
5. In a skillet over medium heat, cook the lamb and onions until the meat is seared. Transfer the softened onions and seared meat to the slow cooker.
6. Pour the can of chopped tomatoes into the slow cooker followed by the plain yoghurt, coriander, and bay leaf. Stir to combine the sauces and mix with the meat.
7. Cover and cook on low for 5-6 hours.
8. Serve alone or with rice.

Poultry & Seafood Main Courses

CREAMY CHICKEN PASTA WITH SUN-DRIED TOMATOES

MAKES 4 SERVINGS
SETTING: HIGH | PREP TIME: 10 MINUTES | COOK TIME: 3.5 HOURS

PER SERVING
CARBS: 54.3G | PROTEIN: 38.6G | FIBRE: 2.3G | FAT: 43.8G
KCAL: 768

INGREDIENTS

- 500ml chicken broth
- 500g boneless chicken thighs
- 250g short pasta of choice
- 220g cream cheese
- 140g sun-dried tomatoes (including oil)
- 50g grated parmesan cheese
- 3 garlic cloves
- 1 red onion
- 1 tbsp Italian seasoning

INSTRUCTIONS

1. Finely dice the red onion and garlic. On a separate chopping board, cut the chicken thighs into bite-sized pieces.
2. Pour the chicken broth into the greased slow cooker. Season the broth with salt, pepper, and Italian seasoning.
3. Add the chicken thighs, onion, and garlic to the slow cooker.
4. Cover with the lid and cook on high for 3 hours or until chicken is cooked through.
5. Add the pasta and sun-dried tomatoes to the slow cooker. Cook on high for 25 more minutes.
6. Add the parmesan and cream cheese to the slow cooker. Stir into the pasta and broth until fully combined.
7. Serve with any extra parmesan cheese.

FISH AU GRATIN

MAKES 6 SERVINGS
SETTING: HIGH | PREP TIME: 10 MINUTES | COOK TIME: 2 HOURS

PER SERVING
CARBS: 7.4G | PROTEIN: 54.4G | FIBRE: 0.5G | FAT: 26.3G
KCAL: 481

INGREDIENTS

- 1.3kg cod or tilapia fillets
- 300ml milk
- 250g shredded cheddar cheese
- 60g butter
- 30g grated parmesan cheese
- 3 tbsps all-purpose flour
- 1 tsp lemon juice
- 1 tsp mustard
- 1 tsp chopped chives (optional)
- 1 lemon (optional)

INSTRUCTIONS

1. Heat a saucepan with butter over medium heat. Add the flour and mustard. Season with salt and pepper. Stir to combine for 2-3 minutes until you have a smooth paste.

2. Pour in the milk one-third at a time, stirring constantly so the sauce can thicken.

3. Add the shredded cheddar cheese and continue to stir until the cheese melts into the sauce. Once all the cheese is in, add the lemon juice.

4. Layer the white fish at the bottom of the slow cooker. Pour in all the cheese sauce until the fish is completely and evenly coated. Top everything with a sprinkling of parmesan cheese.

5. Cover and cook on high for 2 hours.

6. Serve with a topping of chopped chives and lemon wedges on the side.

CHICKEN ENCHILADAS

MAKES 6 SERVINGS (2 EACH)
SETTING: HIGH | PREP TIME: 15 MINUTES | COOK TIME: 3 HOURS

PER SERVING
CARBS: 92.4G | PROTEIN: 57.1G | FIBRE: 33.1G | FAT: 37.7G
KCAL: 921

INGREDIENTS

For the enchiladas:

- 12 small tortillas
- 400g shredded cheddar or mozzarella cheese
- 400g black beans
- 300g shredded chicken (cooked)
- 160g corn
- 100g plum or Roma tomatoes
- 100g green chilli peppers (mild)
- 2 tbsps white or yellow onion (chopped)
- 1 tbsp lime juice

For the sauce:

- 400ml vegetable broth
- 3 tbsps all-purpose flour
- 3 tbsps olive oil
- 2 tbsps tomato paste
- 2 tsps chilli powder*
- 1 tsp apple cider vinegar
- 1 tsp garlic powder
- 1 tsp cumin
- ¼ tsp oregano

* If you're especially sensitive to spice, reduce to 1 tsp. If you're a fan of spice, increase to 3 tsps.

INSTRUCTIONS

1. Start by making the sauce in a pot with olive oil over medium heat. Make sure the pot is hot before adding the ingredients.

2. Add the flour, chilli powder, garlic powder, cumin, and oregano. Season well with salt. Stir constantly for about 1 minute and then add the tomato paste followed by the vegetable broth. Make sure to keep stirring to break up any clumps that form.

3. Bring to a simmer by increasing the heat to medium-high. Try to keep this at a gentle simmer, which may mean reducing the heat slightly. Stir the sauce as it simmers for about 5-6 minutes or until the sauce is nicely thickened.

4. After removing the sauce from heat, stir in the apple cider vinegar. Season with pepper and add more salt if you desire. Now, your sauce is ready.

5. Cover the bottom of the greased slow cooker with one-third of the enchilada sauce.

6. Finely dice the tomatoes.

7. In a bowl, combine another third of the enchilada sauce with the diced tomatoes, shredded chicken, corn, onions, beans, lime juice, and chilli peppers.

8. Divide the mixture evenly between the dozen tortillas. Roll and place into the slow cooker with the seam of the wrap facing down. Create an even layer of about six then top with half of what remains of the sauce.

9. Repeat with the remaining chicken mixture and tortillas. Top the second layer with all of the remaining sauce.

10. Top everything with your chosen shredded cheese.

11. Cover and cook on low for 3 hours.

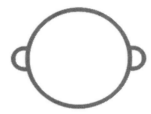

COCONUT CHICKEN CURRY

MAKES 8 SERVINGS
SETTING: LOW | PREP TIME: 15 MINUTES | COOK TIME: 5 HOURS

PER SERVING
CARBS: 20G | PROTEIN: 36.6G | FIBRE: 5.4G | FAT: 34.6G
KCAL: 526

INGREDIENTS

- 900g boneless chicken breasts
- 800ml coconut milk (2 cans)
- 60g tomato paste
- 4 garlic cloves
- 3 sweet potatoes
- 2 onions
- 2 tbsps curry powder
- 1 tbsp olive oil
- 2 tsps paprika
- ½ tsp coriander

INSTRUCTIONS

1. Finely mince the garlic and chop the onions. Peel and slice the sweet potatoes into cubes of about 2-3 cm.

2. On a separate chopping board, slice the chicken breasts into chunks of a similar size to the sweet potatoes.

3. Heat olive oil in a skillet over medium heat. Cook the onions until they look soft and translucent, about 4-5 minutes.

4. Add minced garlic and curry powder to the pan. Cook for 1 more minute, stirring often to prevent burning.

5. Add the garlic and onion mixture to the slow cooker followed by the chopped chicken, sweet potatoes, coconut milk, and tomato paste. Season with salt, pepper, and paprika. Stir to combine all the flavours.

6. Cover and cook on low for 5 hours.

7. Top with coriander and serve alone or with rice.

CITRUS SALMON WITH CREAM SAUCE

MAKES 4 SERVINGS
SETTING: LOW | PREP TIME: 20 MINUTES | COOK TIME: 2 HOURS

PER SERVING
CARBS: 35.6G | PROTEIN: 55.3G | FIBRE: 2.1G | FAT: 30.2G
KCAL: 615

INGREDIENTS

For the salmon:

- 1kg salmon fillets
- 250ml vegetable broth
- 60g butter (melted)
- 3 garlic cloves
- 3 shallots

- 2 lemons
- 1 orange
- 1 tsp thyme
- ½ tsp cayenne pepper

For the sauce:

- 150ml double cream
- 100ml water or chicken broth

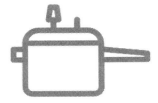

INSTRUCTIONS

1. Mince the garlic and shallots. Zest the lemons and orange. Chop one of the lemons into slices and the orange into halves.
2. Line the slow cooker with parchment paper then create a layer of lemon slices at the bottom.
3. Insert the salmon into the slow cooker on top of the lemon slices.
4. In a bowl, combine the melted butter, minced garlic, shallots, cayenne pepper, and thyme. Season with salt and pepper. Add most of the lemon and orange zest, saving a pinch of each to use in the sauce. Mix together.
5. Pour the butter, zest, and spice mixture over the salmon in the slow cooker.
6. Pour the vegetable broth around the salmon, not on top.
7. Cover and cook on low for 2 hours.
8. About 15-20 minutes before the salmon is done, begin making the cream sauce. Heat a small saucepan over medium-high heat.
9. Add the cream, water or chicken broth, the juice of one whole lemon, and the juice of half an orange. Stir to fully combine.
10. Reduce to low heat, cover, and allow to simmer for 7-10 minutes.
11. Increase to medium-high heat. Add the remaining lemon and orange zest. Season with salt and pepper. Cook for 1-2 more minutes or until the sauce looks like it has thickened.
12. Serve the salmon with sauce on the side or on top.

CHICKEN CACCIATORE

MAKES 4 SERVINGS
SETTING: LOW | PREP TIME: 10 MINUTES | COOK TIME: 8 HOURS

PER SERVING
CARBS: 11.4G | PROTEIN: 51.4G | FIBRE: 3.1G | FAT: 14.6G
KCAL: 392

INGREDIENTS

- 1kg chicken thighs
- 800g chopped tomatoes (2 cans)
- 250g mushrooms
- 100g pitted kalamata olives
- 60ml red wine or chicken broth
- 3 garlic cloves
- 2 bell peppers
- 2 tsps basil

INSTRUCTIONS

1. Mince the garlic and chop the bell peppers. Quarter-slice the mushrooms.
2. Season both sides of all the chicken thighs with salt and pepper.
3. Add the seasoned chicken thighs to the slow cooker followed by the minced garlic, sliced bell peppers, mushrooms, chopped tomatoes, and red wine or chicken broth. Season with salt, pepper, and basil.
4. Cover and cook on low for 7-8 hours until the chicken is fully cooked.
5. Once cooked, add the pitted olives and mix in.
6. Serve alone or with pasta.

SWEET POTATO TURKEY CHILLI

MAKES 6 SERVINGS
SETTING: LOW | PREP TIME: 10 MINUTES | COOK TIME: 4 HOURS

PER SERVING
CARBS: 59.6G | PROTEIN: 41.6G | FIBRE: 18.4G | FAT: 15.8G
KCAL: 537

INGREDIENTS

- 450g ground turkey
- 400ml chicken broth
- 400g sweet potato puree or mash
- 400g green chilli peppers (1 can)
- 400g cannellini beans (1 can)
- 180g sour cream
- 1 onion
- 1 tsp garlic powder
- 1 tsp chilli powder
- 1 tsp cumin

INSTRUCTIONS

1. Prepare by dicing the onion.
2. Heat a skillet over medium heat. Cook the ground turkey and diced onions until the meat is lightly browned, about 5-6 minutes. Use the spatula or spoon to break up the turkey so it doesn't cook in clumps.
3. Drain any excess water from the pan then transfer the onions and turkey to the slow cooker.
4. Pour the chicken broth and sweet potato puree into the slow cooker. Next, add the green chilli peppers. Season with salt, pepper, garlic powder, chilli powder, and cumin.
5. Cover and cook on low for 4 hours.
6. Add the can of beans and cook for 1 more hour.
7. Serve with sour cream.

CHICKEN MARSALA

MAKES 4 SERVINGS
SETTING: LOW, HIGH | PREP TIME: 10 MINUTES |
COOK TIME: 5 HOURS 40 MINUTES

PER SERVING
CARBS: 11.1G | PROTEIN: 53.1G | FIBRE: 0.9G | FAT: 22.3G
KCAL: 492

INGREDIENTS

- 700g boneless chicken breasts
- 250g mushrooms
- 150ml dry marsala wine*
- 60ml double cream
- 30g cornstarch
- 2 garlic cloves

- 2 tbsps parsley
- 1 tbsp olive oil
- 1 tsp basil
- 1 tsp thyme
- 100ml water

* Can be substituted with dry white wine or a dark sherry.

INSTRUCTIONS

1. Mince the garlic and slice the mushrooms. On a separate chopping board, season the chicken breasts with salt, pepper, thyme, and basil.

2. Heat a skillet with olive oil over medium-high heat. Cook the chicken until lightly browned, about 3-4 minutes per side.

3. Transfer the seared chicken to the slow cooker followed by the garlic, wine, and sliced mushrooms.

4. Cover and cook on low for 5 hours.

5. In a small bowl, whisk the water and cornstarch together until blended.

6. Remove the chicken breasts from the slow cooker. Pour in the cornstarch mixture and the double cream. Stir or whisk to combine with the wine.

7. Once finished, add the chicken back to the slow cooker. Cover and cook on high for 20-30 minutes or until the sauce has thickened.

8. Top with parsley and serve.

Vegetarian Main Courses

GREEN LENTIL CURRY

MAKES 6 SERVINGS
SETTING: HIGH | PREP TIME: 10 MINUTES | COOK TIME: 4 HOURS

PER SERVING
CARBS: 51.9G | PROTEIN: 21.7G | FIBRE: 23.3G | FAT: 19.9G
KCAL: 461

INGREDIENTS

- 400ml coconut milk
- 400g chopped tomatoes (1 can)
- 400g green lentils
- 200g plain yoghurt
- 5 garlic cloves
- 1 onion
- 1 tbsp olive oil
- 1 tsp cumin
- 1 tsp coriander
- 1 tsp turmeric powder
- 1 tsp cayenne pepper
- 500ml water

INSTRUCTIONS

1. Dice the onion and garlic.
2. Heat a small skillet over medium-low heat. Cook the onion and garlic for 4-5 minutes until lightly golden.
3. Add the turmeric powder, cayenne pepper, coriander and cumin. Season with salt and stir for 20-30 seconds.
4. Transfer the cooked garlic, onion, and spices to the slow cooker.
5. Pour in the coconut milk, chopped tomatoes, water, and lentils. Mix together.
6. Cover and cook on high for 4 hours.
7. Serve alone or with rice.

BUTTERNUT SQUASH MAC & CHEESE

MAKES 6 SERVINGS
SETTING: HIGH | PREP TIME: 15 MINUTES | COOK TIME: 4 HOURS

PER SERVING
CARBS: 73.9 | PROTEIN: 31.1G | FIBRE: 4.3G | FAT: 20.8G
KCAL: 605

INGREDIENTS

- 500g macaroni or other short pasta
- 350g butternut squash (cubed)
- 200ml vegetable broth
- 150g shredded sharp cheddar cheese
- 150g grated gouda or gruyere cheese
- 150ml milk
- 1 garlic clove
- 1 onion
- ¼ tsp red pepper flakes
- ¼ tsp thyme
- 100g grated parmesan cheese (optional)

INSTRUCTIONS

1. Mince the garlic and dice the onion.
2. Heat olive oil in a skillet over medium heat. Cook the garlic and onion for 2-3 minutes until fragrant and tender.
3. Add the cooked garlic and onion to the slow cooker followed by the broth and cubed butternut squash. Stir together.
4. Cover and cook on high for 4 hours.
5. About 10-15 minutes before cooking time is complete, start making the pasta. Bring a pot of water to boil and cook the pasta till they're al dente.
6. Once the squash is cooked and tender, use a blender or potato masher to create a smooth paste.
7. Add the shredded cheese and milk. Season with salt, pepper, thyme, and red pepper flakes. Stir to fully combine.
8. Add the cooked pasta to the cheesy squash sauce.
9. Serve with grated parmesan cheese.

STUFFED BELL PEPPERS

MAKES 3 SERVINGS (2 EACH)
SETTING: LOW | PREP TIME: 5 MINUTES | COOK TIME: 4 HOURS

PER SERVING
CARBS: 51.6G | PROTEIN: 20.2G | FIBRE: 14.7G | FAT: 20.8G
KCAL: 455

INGREDIENTS

- 6 red or yellow bell peppers
- 400g black beans (1 can)
- 400g diced tomatoes (1 can)
- 180g quinoa (uncooked)
- 80g shredded cheddar cheese
- 60g corn
- 1 onion
- ½ tsp cumin
- ½ tsp chilli powder
- 150g sour cream or plain Greek yoghurt (optional)

INSTRUCTIONS

1. Prepare by dicing the onion and slicing the stems from the peppers. Carefully remove the seeds.
2. In a bowl, combine the quinoa, black beans, corn, onion, diced tomatoes, chilli powder, cumin, and three-quarters of the shredded cheddar cheese. Season with salt and mix together.
3. Spoon into the peppers until completely full.
4. Pour about 100ml into the greased slow cooker.
5. Place the stuffed peppers into the slow cooker and arrange so they are not touching.
6. Cover and cook on low for 4 hours.
7. Serve with sour cream or plain yoghurt as a topping or dipping sauce.

VEGETABLE CURRY

MAKES 6 SERVINGS
SETTING: LOW | PREP TIME: 15 MINUTES | COOK TIME: 5 HOURS

PER SERVING
CARBS: 59.3G | PROTEIN: 17.5G | FIBRE: 15.9G | FAT: 13G
KCAL: 406

INGREDIENTS

- 400ml vegetable broth
- 400g chickpeas (1 can)
- 200ml coconut milk
- 200g cauliflower
- 200g sweet potato
- 3 yellow or red bell peppers
- 2 tbsps tomato paste
- 1 tbsp olive or canola oil
- 2 garlic cloves
- 1 onion
- 2 tsps ground coriander
- 1 tsp turmeric powder
- ½ tsp cayenne pepper
- ½ tsp ground ginger

INSTRUCTIONS

1. Prepare by mincing the garlic and dicing the onion. Chop the sweet potatoes into cubes, the cauliflower into florets, and dice the bell peppers.

2. Heat a pan with oil over medium-high heat. Cook the diced onions for 4-5 minutes until translucent and lightly golden.

3. Add the minced garlic, coriander, turmeric, cayenne pepper, ground ginger, and tomato paste. Stir to combine and cook for 1 minute or until the garlic is fragrant.

4. Transfer the mixture of onions, garlic, and spices to the slow cooker.

5. Pour in the vegetable broth, coconut milk, and all the chopped vegetables.

6. Mash the chickpeas with a fork, potato masher, or for speed and use, use a food processor.

7. Transfer the mashed chickpeas into the slow cooker. Season with salt and pepper. Stir the contents of the slow cooker to fully mix.

8. Cover and cook on low for 5 hours.

9. Serve alone or with rice.

AUBERGINE, OLIVE & RAISIN TAGINE

MAKES 5 SERVINGS
SETTING: LOW | PREP TIME: 10 MINUTES | COOK TIME: 2 HOURS 40 MINUTES

PER SERVING
CARBS: 34.3G | PROTEIN: 7.6G | FIBRE: 11.9G | FAT: 19.2G
KCAL: 312

INGREDIENTS

- 700ml vegetable broth
- 400g pitted green olives (1 jar)
- 60g raisins
- 5 garlic cloves
- 2 aubergines
- 2 white onions
- 4 tbsps olive oil
- 2 tbsps cumin
- 2 tbsps paprika
- 1 tbsp coriander
- 1 tbsp chilli powder
- 1 tsp red wine vinegar
- 1 tsp cayenne pepper
- 1 tsp turmeric

INSTRUCTIONS

1. Finely mince the garlic and dice the onions. Slice the aubergines lengthwise and then halve into thin strips. Rub salt into the aubergines to draw out any bitter moisture. Drain the water or oil out of the jar of olives.

2. In a bowl, combine the cumin, paprika, chilli powder, vinegar, cayenne pepper, turmeric, garlic, and three-quarters of the olive oil (3 tablespoons).

3. Heat a large skillet with the remaining olive oil (1 tablespoon) over medium heat and cook the onions for about 6-7 minutes.

4. Add the spice blend to the pan and cook for 1 more minute until the garlic is nicely fragrant.

5. Pour the vegetable broth into the slow cooker. Add the sliced aubergines, raisins, seasoned onions, and olives to the slow cooker. Season with salt, pepper, and coriander. Stir well to fully combine.

6. Cover and cook on low for 2.5 hours, making sure to stir twice over the course of that time.

7. Serve alone or with couscous.

EASY RATATOUILLE

MAKES 6 SERVINGS
SETTING: LOW | PREP TIME: 20 MINUTES | COOK TIME: 7 HOURS

PER SERVING
CARBS: 59.4G | PROTEIN: 11.3G | FIBRE: 11.7G | FAT: 7.4G
KCAL: 320

INGREDIENTS

- 650g baking potatoes
- 150g tomato paste
- 50g grated parmesan cheese
- 3 courgettes
- 3 garlic cloves
- 2 red or green bell peppers
- 2 aubergines
- 1 sweet potato
- 1 red onion
- 2 tbsps olive oil
- ½ tsp oregano

INSTRUCTIONS

1. Mince the garlic. Slice the courgettes and aubergines into rounds of 1cm thickness. Finely slice the potatoes, peeled sweet potato, aubergines, onion, and bell peppers into thinner rounds of about 0.25 cm.

2. In your greased slow cooker, arrange the vegetable rounds into a circle or oval along the inside edge of your machine. Do this in a repeating order. For example, sweet potato followed by regular potato, courgette, aubergine, bell pepper, and onion.

3. Once the outer edge is complete, continue with another ring of vegetable rounds on the inside until the bottom of the machine is covered.

4. After a layer of vegetables is complete, season with salt, pepper, and oregano, and add some minced garlic. Spread half of the tomato paste over the layer.

5. Continue with a second layer until all vegetables are finished, topping with spices and tomato paste at the end.

6. Cover and cook on low for 7 hours.

7. Serve with a topping of grated parmesan cheese.

CHICKPEA PEANUT STEW

MAKES 6 SERVINGS
SETTING: HIGH | PREP TIME: 5 MINUTES | COOK TIME: 6 HOURS 15 MINUTES

PER SERVING
CARBS: 58G | PROTEIN: 23.8G | FIBRE: 15.8G | FAT: 17.7G
KCAL: 467

INGREDIENTS

- 800ml vegetable broth
- 400g chickpeas (1 can)
- 400g chopped tomatoes (1 can)
- 150g peanut butter
- 80g spinach
- 4 garlic cloves
- 2 sweet potatoes
- 1 onion
- 1 tsp cumin
- 1 tsp coriander
- ½ tsp cayenne pepper

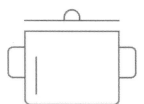

INSTRUCTIONS

1. Dice the onion and mince the garlic. Peel and cube the sweet potatoes into pieces of about 3-4cm.

2. Add the broth, drained chickpeas, chopped tomatoes, sweet potatoes, peanut butter, onions, and garlic to the slow cooker. Season with salt, cumin, coriander, and cayenne pepper. Stir to fully combine all ingredients.

3. Cover and cook on low for 6 hours.

4. Add spinach to the cooked stew. Cook on high for another 10-15 minutes or until the spinach looks wilted.

5. Serve alone or with bread or rice.

VEGETARIAN JAMBALAYA

MAKES 6 SERVINGS
SETTING: LOW, HIGH | PREP TIME: 10 MINUTES | COOK TIME: 6 HOURS

PER SERVING
CARBS: 105G | PROTEIN: 21.3G | FIBRE: 14G | FAT: 3.8G
KCAL: 538

INGREDIENTS

- 1ltr vegetable broth
- 400g chopped tomatoes (1 can)
- 400g red kidney beans (1 can)
- 400g long grain rice
- 4 garlic cloves
- 2 stalks celery
- 2 spring onions
- 1 green bell pepper
- 1 red bell pepper
- 1 onion
- 1 tbsp olive oil
- 2 tsps Worcestershire sauce
- 1 tsp thyme
- 1 tsp oregano
- 1 tsp cayenne pepper
- ½ tsp red pepper flakes

INSTRUCTIONS

1. Dice the onion, garlic, bell peppers, and celery. Finely slice the spring onions. Add all except the spring onions to the slow cooker.

2. Pour the chopped tomatoes, red kidney beans, Worcestershire sauce, olive oil, and vegetable broth into the slow cooker. Season with salt, pepper, thyme, oregano, cayenne pepper, and red pepper flakes. Stir to combine all ingredients.

3. Cover and cook on low for 4-5 hours.

4. Add the rice to the slow cooker. Cook on high for 1 more hour or until the rice looks tender.

5. Stir in the kidney beans.

6. Top with sliced spring onions and serve.

Side Dishes

GLAZED CARROTS

MAKES 6 SERVINGS
SETTING: LOW | PREP TIME: 5 MINUTES | COOK TIME: 7 HOURS

PER SERVING
CARBS: 24.4G | PROTEIN: 1.3G | FIBRE: 4.6G | FAT: 13.8G
KCAL: 220

INGREDIENTS

- 900g small carrots
- 100g butter
- 60g peach or apricot preserves
- 50g brown sugar
- 2 tbsps cornstarch
- 2 tbsps water
- ¼ tsp balsamic vinegar
- ¼ tsp thyme

INSTRUCTIONS

1. Layer the small carrots at the bottom of the slow cooker.
2. In a bowl, combine the fruit preserves, sugar, cinnamon, and butter. Season well with salt and pepper.
3. In a separate bowl or cup, stir together the cornstarch and water until combined, then mix into the buttery preserves mixture.
4. Pour the sauce over the carrots in the slow cooker.
5. Cover with the lid and cook on low for about 6-7 hours.

CHEESY SPINACH

MAKES 6 SERVINGS
SETTING: HIGH, LOW | PREP TIME: 5 MINUTES | COOK TIME: 4 HOURS

PER SERVING
CARBS: 9.7G | PROTEIN: 21.2G | FIBRE: 2.2G | FAT: 21.4G
KCAL: 311

INGREDIENTS

- 550g spinach (chopped and thawed)
- 300g cottage cheese
- 200g shredded cheddar cheese
- 50g butter
- 30g all-purpose flour
- 3 large eggs
- ½ tsp garlic powder

INSTRUCTIONS

1. Combine all the ingredients. Season well with salt and pepper.
2. Pour into a greased slow cooker and cover.
3. Cook on high for 1 hour.*
4. Reduce heat to low and cook for 3 more hours.

* Alternatively, cook on low for 4 hours for a total of 7 hours cook time.

CREAMED CORN WITH BACON

MAKES 6 SERVINGS
SETTING: HIGH | PREP TIME: 5 MINUTES | COOK TIME: 3 HOURS

PER SERVING
CARBS: 10.3G | PROTEIN: 4.9G | FIBRE: 0.9G | FAT: 33.5G
KCAL: 351

INGREDIENTS

- 1.2kg sweet corn (6 cans)
- 220g cream cheese
- 100ml milk
- 100ml double cream
- 100g butter
- 3 bacon strips (cooked)
- 1 spring onion
- 1 tbsp granulated sugar

INSTRUCTIONS

1. Combine all ingredients in the slow cooker except for the bacon and onion. Season with salt and a generous amount of black pepper. Stir to combine.
2. Cover and cook on high for 3 hours.
3. Shortly before cooking time is complete, uncover and stir the contents of the slow cooker then allow to cook as normal.
4. While the corn is still in the slow cooker, finely chop the spring onions. Crumble the cooked bacon or slice into tiny pieces of about 1cm.
5. Scatter the bacon bits all over the cooked creamed corn.
6. Serve with a topping of spring onions.

SWEET BRUSSELS SPROUTS WITH CRANBERRIES & FETA

MAKES 6 SERVINGS
SETTING: HIGH | PREP TIME: 5 MINUTES | COOK TIME: 2 HOURS

PER SERVING
CARBS: 25.8G | PROTEIN: 8.1G | FIBRE: 6.7G | FAT: 6.4G
KCAL: 175

INGREDIENTS

- 900g Brussels sprouts
- 100g feta cheese crumbles
- 100g cranberries
- 90g maple syrup
- 1 tbsp olive oil

INSTRUCTIONS

1. Trim and halve the Brussels sprouts.
2. Add the chopped sprouts to the slow cooker.
3. Season well with salt and pepper. Toss with maple syrup and olive oil.
4. Cover and cook on high for 2 hours.
5. Toss the cooked sprouts with cranberries.
6. Serve with a topping of feta cheese crumbles.

GREEN BEAN CASSEROLE

MAKES 6 SERVINGS
SETTING: LOW | PREP TIME: 5 MINUTES | COOK TIME: 2 HOURS

PER SERVING
CARBS: 27.2G | PROTEIN: 13.5G | FIBRE: 3.4G | FAT: 36.5G
KCAL: 449

INGREDIENTS

- 1kg green beans
- 400ml cream of mushroom soup (1 can)
- 200ml sour cream
- 200ml milk
- 200g Fudco Crispy Fried Onions (1 canister)
- 80g grated parmesan cheese
- ½ tsp garlic powder

INSTRUCTIONS

1. Add the green beans to the greased slow cooker.
2. In a bowl, add the mushroom soup, sour cream, milk, and garlic powder. Season well with salt and pepper. Whisk to fully combine.
3. Pour over the green beans in the slow cooker. Add the grated parmesan cheese, half of the fried onions, and mix together.
4. Cover and cook on low for 2 hours.
5. Shortly before cook time is complete, heat a skillet on the stove at medium-high heat. Add the rest of the fried onions. Cook until the onions are nicely browned, about 3 minutes. Stir constantly.
6. Serve with the topping of pan-crisped onions.

GARLIC HERB MASHED POTATOES

MAKES 6 SERVINGS
SETTING: HIGH | PREP TIME: 10 MINUTES | COOK TIME: 2 HOURS

PER SERVING
CARBS: 8.1G | PROTEIN: 2.2G | FIBRE: 0.5G | FAT: 14.7G
KCAL: 168

INGREDIENTS

- 1.1kg baking or red potatoes
- 130g sour cream or plain yoghurt
- 110ml whole milk
- 70g butter
- 4 garlic cloves
- 3 tsps parsley
- ¼ tsp oregano

INSTRUCTIONS

1. Chop potatoes into small chunks of about 4-5 cm. No need to peel them. Mince the garlic cloves.
2. Add the chopped potatoes to a greased slow cooker. Cover and cook on high for 2 hours or until the potatoes are tender.
3. Once the potatoes are softened, add all the remaining ingredients to the slow cooker. Season well with salt and pepper.
4. With a masher or vigorously with a wooden spoon, mash the potatoes and fully combine with all other ingredients.
5. Serve alone or with an extra dollop of butter on top.

BEANS & VEGETABLES

MAKES 8 SERVINGS
SETTING: LOW | PREP TIME: 10 MINUTES | COOK TIME: 4 HOURS

PER SERVING
CARBS: 96.2G | PROTEIN: 37.1G | FIBRE: 39G | FAT: 1.6G
KCAL: 532

INGREDIENTS

- 1.2kg cannellini beans (drained)
- 200ml vegetable broth
- 150g spinach
- 60g sun-dried tomatoes
- 5 garlic cloves
- 4 medium carrots
- 1 onion
- 2 tsps cumin
- 2 tsps coriander
- 2 tsps parsley

INSTRUCTIONS

1. Coarsely chop the spinach and onion. Dice the garlic and carrots.
2. Add the cannellini beans, broth, diced garlic, onion, and carrots to the slow cooker. Season with salt, pepper, and cumin. Mix together.
3. Cover and cook on low for 4 hours.
4. Add the chopped spinach and tomatoes. Cook for another 15 minutes.
5. Season with coriander and parsley, and serve.

SPICY CAULIFLOWER & POTATOES

MAKES 6 SERVINGS
SETTING: LOW, HIGH | PREP TIME: 15 MINUTES |
COOK TIME: 4 HOURS 10 MINUTES

PER SERVING
CARBS: 41.4G | PROTEIN: 8.2G | FIBRE: 8.6G | FAT: 8.3G
KCAL: 255

INGREDIENTS

- 900g baking or red potatoes
- 500g cauliflower
- 400g chopped tomatoes (1 can)
- 150g spinach
- 150g sour cream
- 3 plum tomatoes
- 2 yellow onions
- 2 tbsps curry powder
- 1 tbsp butter
- 1 tbsp coriander
- 2 tsps chilli powder

INSTRUCTIONS

1. Dice the plum tomatoes and onions. Chop the cauliflower into bite-sized florets and the potatoes into halves or quarters.

2. Heat the butter in a pan over medium heat. Cook the onions until softened and translucent, about 4-5 minutes.

3. Add the can of chopped tomatoes followed by the curry powder and chilli powder. Stir to combine.

4. Raise the heat to bring the curry tomato mixture to a boil, then allow to simmer for 5 minutes.

5. Add the chopped potatoes and cauliflower florets to the greased slow cooker, then pour in the curry tomato mixture. Season with salt and pepper.

6. Cover and cook on low for 4 hours or until the vegetables are tender.

7. Add the spinach, diced plum tomatoes, and coriander. Cook on high for 10 more minutes.

8. Top with sour cream and serve.

Desserts

STICKY TOFFEE PUDDING

MAKES 10 SERVINGS
SETTING: LOW | PREP TIME: 20 MINUTES | COOK TIME: 4 HOURS

PER SERVING
CARBS: 92.8G | PROTEIN: 8.3G | FIBRE: 2.6G | FAT: 26G
KCAL: 627

INGREDIENTS

For the cake:

- 500g all-purpose flour
- 200ml milk
- 200ml water
- 150g dates (chopped and pitted)
- 130g unsalted butter (softened)
- 120g sugar
- 2 large eggs
- 1 tsp vanilla extract
- 1 tsp baking soda

For the sauce:

- 300ml heavy cream
- 300g brown sugar
- 2 tbsps unsalted butter

INSTRUCTIONS

1. Start by making the sauce in a saucepan over medium heat. Add the heavy cream, brown sugar, and unsalted butter to the pan. Stir until the sugar is dissolved then reduce heat to medium-low. Allow to simmer for 4-5 minutes.

2. In a separate pan, boil the chopped dates and water. Once the water is hot, add a quarter of the baking soda and stir to combine. Allow to cool once done.

3. Add the remainder of the baking soda to a mixing bowl with flour.

4. With an electric mixer or whisking vigorously with a fork, cream the sugar, butter, and vanilla extract. Slowly add the eggs followed by the flour and baking soda, milk, and lastly, the watery date mixture.

5. Pour the batter into the greased slow cooker and coat entirely with the sauce.

6. Cover and cook on low for 3-4 hours.

HOT FUDGE CHOCOLATE CAKE

MAKES 8 SERVINGS
SETTING: HIGH | PREP TIME: 40 MINUTES | COOK TIME: 2 HOURS 30 MINUTES

PER SERVING
CARBS: 92.3G | PROTEIN: 6.6G | FIBRE: 4.3G | FAT: 14.2G
KCAL: 495

INGREDIENTS

- 250g all-purpose flour
- 250ml whole milk
- 200g granulated sugar
- 200g brown sugar
- 150g semi-sweet chocolate chips
- 75g cocoa powder
- 60ml canola or vegetable oil
- 4 tsps baking powder
- 1 tsp vanilla extract
- 700ml hot water

INSTRUCTIONS

1. In a mixing bowl, combine the sugar, flour, baking powder, and 4 tablespoons of the cocoa powder. Add a pinch of salt.

2. Combine with the vanilla extract, whole milk, and oil. Stir well to fully mix together.

3. Transfer the batter to a greased slow cooker, creating an even layer at the bottom. Scatter the chocolate chips evenly across the batter.

4. In a large bowl, combine the remaining cocoa powder with the brown sugar. Carefully pour in the hot water. Stir until the mixture is smooth.

5. Pour this mixture over the batter in the slow cooker, but do not stir.

6. Cover and cook on high for 1.5 to 2.5 hours.

7. Allow to cool for 30 minutes, then serve alone or with ice cream.

BAKED APPLES

MAKES 5 SERVINGS (1 EACH)
SETTING: HIGH | PREP TIME: 10 MINUTES | COOK TIME: 2 HOURS 30 MINUTES

PER SERVING
CARBS: 50.8G | PROTEIN: 2.8G | FIBRE: 7.5G | FAT: 16.6G
KCAL: 342

INGREDIENTS

- 5 red apples
- 60g butter (melted)
- 60g brown sugar
- 50g old-fashioned oats
- 40g chopped pecans
- 1 tsp ground cinnamon
- 100ml water

INSTRUCTIONS

1. Remove the cores from the apples using a sharp knife or an apple corer. With a knife, create a wider well at the top of the apple by removing more apple flesh. This ensures you can fit more toppings in it.
2. In a bowl, combine the butter, oats, chopped pecans, ground cinnamon, sugar, and a pinch of salt.
3. Stuff the empty apple till it is completely full. Press down to pack it in more tightly if necessary.
4. Pour water into the slow cooker then set down the stuffed apples inside.
5. Cover and cook on high for 2.5 hours.
6. Serve alone or with ice cream and caramel sauce.

CINNAMON ROLLS

MAKES 8 SERVINGS
SETTING: HIGH | PREP TIME: 30 MINUTES | COOK TIME: 2 HOURS

PER SERVING
CARBS: 62.9G | PROTEIN: 7.2G | FIBRE: 2G | FAT: 15.2G
KCAL: 412

INGREDIENTS

For the dough:

- 350g all-purpose flour
- 200ml whole milk
- 60g granulated sugar
- 60g butter
- 1 egg
- 2 ¼ tsp instant or active yeast (1 packet)

For the filling:

- 70g granulated sugar
- 70g butter (softened)
- 4 tsps ground cinnamon

For the icing:

- 150g icing sugar
- 40ml whole milk
- 1 tsp vanilla extract

INSTRUCTIONS

1. Prepare for the dough by heating the butter and milk in a saucepan over low heat.

2. Once warmed, transfer the milk and butter mixture to a mixing bowl. Add the instant yeast and roughly 1 teaspoon of sugar. Whisk to combine.

3. Cover the bowl and allow to sit for about 7-10 minutes until the yeast and dissolves and begins to form a foam. If this does not happen, start over with a new packet of instant yeast.

4. Add the remaining sugar for the dough, butter, egg, a pinch of salt, and about two-thirds of the flour. Use a hand mixer to combine or whisk vigorously with a fork or whisk.

5. As you continue to whisk, slowly add the remaining flour until you have a soft dough. If you don't have a hand mixer, it may be easier to use a wooden spoon at this point. If the dough keeps sticking to the side of the bowl, add a teaspoon of extra flour at a time until this problem is resolved.

6. Spread the dough out on a lightly floured surface. Roll into a rectangle of about 1 to 1.5 cm thickness. Knead for 45 seconds to 1 minute. Allow to rest for 10 minutes.

7. Start with the filling by making a layer of softened butter over the dough.

8. In a bowl, combine the sugar and ground cinnamon then scatter over the layer of softened butter.

9. Roll the dough rectangle tightly into a long log, then slice into even pieces. It should make between 10-12 pieces.

10. Line your slow cooker with parchment paper or grease with cooking spray or butter. Place the uncooked rolls into the machine.

11. Insert a paper towel under the lid of your slow cooker. This ensures that condensation doesn't drip onto the rolls while they are cooking.

12. Cover and cook on high for 2 hours.

13. Remove immediately after cooking time is complete by lifting the parchment paper out of the machine.

14. Start making the icing by whisking the icing sugar, milk, and vanilla extract. Feel free to add more milk if you would like a thinner glaze.

15. Drizzle icing over the freshly cooked cinnamon rolls and serve.

APPLE PUDDING CAKE

MAKES 8 SERVINGS
SETTING: HIGH | PREP TIME: 15 MINUTES | COOK TIME: 2 HOURS

PER SERVING
CARBS: 85G | PROTEIN: 4.6G | FIBRE: 3.8G | FAT: 4.3G
KCAL: 382

INGREDIENTS

- 350ml orange juice
- 240g all-purpose flour
- 200ml whole milk
- 200g granulated sugar
- 120g brown sugar or honey
- 4 red apples
- 2 tbsps butter (melted)
- 3 tsps baking powder
- 1 tsp ground cinnamon

INSTRUCTIONS

1. Core, peel, and dice the apples.

2. Add about three-quarters of the sugar (150g) to a mixing bowl. Combine with flour, baking powder, and a pinch of salt.

3. Mix the melted butter into the bowl until you have a coarse mixture, then stir in the milk to moisten.

4. With a spoon, add the batter to the bottom of the greased slow cooker until you have an even layer.

5. Create an even layer of diced apples on top.

6. In another bowl, combine the melted butter, honey, orange juice, ground cinnamon, and all the remaining sugar. Whisk or stir vigorously to combine.

7. Pour this mixture over the diced apples in the slow cooker.

8. Cover and cook on high for 2 hours or until the apples are fork tender.

9. Serve alone or with vanilla ice cream.

BLUEBERRY COBBLER

MAKES 6 SERVINGS
SETTING: LOW | PREP TIME: 5 MINUTES | COOK TIME: 4 HOURS

PER SERVING
CARBS: 68.6G | PROTEIN: 5.4G | FIBRE: 3.7G | FAT: 10.1G
KCAL: 374

INGREDIENTS

- 600g blueberries
- 250ml whole milk
- 180g all-purpose flour
- 150g granulated sugar
- 60g butter (softened)

- 2 tbsps cornstarch
- 3 tsps baking powder
- 2 tsps ground cinnamon
- 1 tsp vanilla extract

INSTRUCTIONS

1. In a bowl, sift together the flour and baking powder. Add two-thirds of the sugar, softened butter, and a pinch of salt.
2. Stir in the milk and mix slowly to prevent clumps from forming.
3. In a separate bowl, combine the remaining one-third of sugar, vanilla extract, ground cinnamon, and blueberries. Mix together so all the blueberries are coated.
4. Add the batter to the greased slow cooker in an even layer. Top with the sugar-coated blueberries.
5. Cook on low for 4 hours.
6. Serve alone or with vanilla ice cream.

SALTED CARAMEL CRUMBLE BARS

MAKES 10 SERVINGS
SETTING: LOW | PREP TIME: 10 MINUTES | COOK TIME: 2 HOURS

PER SERVING
CARBS: 70G | PROTEIN: 5.6G | FIBRE: 0.8G | FAT: 23.9G
KCAL: 506

INGREDIENTS

- 350g caramel
- 300g all-purpose flour
- 250g unsalted butter (softened)
- 200g granulated sugar
- 1 large egg
- 1 tsp vanilla extract
- 1 tsp sea salt

INSTRUCTIONS

1. In a bowl, combine the softened butter, sugar, and vanilla extract using a hand mixer or a fork.
2. Add the egg followed by a pinch of salt. Beat to fully combine.
3. Slowly mix in the flour until a dough forms. You may need to do this one cup at a time.
4. Roll the dough into a ball and separate into two rough halves, with one slightly larger than the other. For ease, rub some dough on your palms so the dough is easier to work with and doesn't stick to your skin.
5. Take the slightly larger piece of dough and press into the bottom of the slow cooker to make the base.
6. Create an even layer of caramel on top of the dough base.
7. Crumble the remaining dough on top of the caramel.
8. Scatter the sea salt over everything, taking care to spread it evenly so it's not too salty in one area.
9. Cover and cook on low for about 2 hours.

Disclaimer

This book contains opinions and ideas of the author and is meant to teach the reader informative and helpful knowledge while due care should be taken by the user in the application of the information provided. The instructions and strategies are possibly not right for every reader and there is no guarantee that they work for everyone. Using this book and implementing the information/recipes therein contained is explicitly your own responsibility and risk. This work with all its contents, does not guarantee correctness, completion, quality or correctness of the provided information. Misinformation or misprints cannot be completely eliminated.

Printed in Great Britain
by Amazon